# the pure and simple home

OU  BAHOLYODHIN

**dbp**

DUNCAN BAIRD PUBLISHERS

LONDON

# the pure and simple home

Ou Baholyodhin

First published as Living with Zen in the United Kingdom and
Ireland by Duncan Baird Publishers in 2000.
This edition published by
Duncan Baird Publishers Ltd
Sixth Floor, Castle House
75–76 Wells Street
London W1T 3QH

Conceived, created and designed by Duncan Baird Publishers

Managing Designer: Manisha Patel
Picture Researcher: Nadine Bazar
Editorial Consultant: Esther Selsdon
Managing Editor: Judy Dean
Editor: Georgina Harris

British Library Cataloguing-in-Publication Data: A catalogue record
for this book is available from the British Library

10 9 8 7 6 5 4 3 2 1

ISBN: 1-84483-062-4

Typeset in Bell Gothic
Colour reproduction by Colourscan, Singapore
Printed by Imago, Singapore

Note: The abbreviations BCE and CE are used in this book:
BCE (Before the Common Era) is the equivalent of BC,
CE (Common Era) the equivalent of AD.

to my Mother, for my life

# contents

# introduction

by Ou Baholyodhin

## joy and happiness

As I see it, there are two ways to achieve joy and happiness. One way is to enhance the sensual beauty of our surroundings. Another is to remove everything that clouds them.

By paring things down to their essentials, we arrive at a clarity which enables us to cope.

Complexity can create a dramatic impression, but simplicity allows us to focus and to appreciate with a profound and touching sensitivity.

I used to have an insatiable hunger for objects, furniture, decorative items for the home, in fact just about anything I could lay my hands on – Victorian kitchen utensils, Art Deco ceramics, mid-twentieth-century design classics, Chinese lacquerware. Every corner of the home was filled with the bizarre and the indefinable, the antique and the modern, the kitsch and the cool. These I carefully arranged to form an eloquent composition.

Today, if I needed to move, I could probably fit all my belongings into a suitcase. Over the years, I seem to have

developed an enthusiasm for stripping myself of once-cherished objects. I ask myself if life would be less without a certain object, and if the answer is no, then out it goes, without any regrets. This is by no means a conscious effort on my part to achieve the minimalist dream, but rather a strong urge from within.

## sense and spirit

Stimulation comes from our surroundings. Tranquility comes from within oneself. I suppose this is how I enjoy living with fewer objects in my life.

I believe that every object has a soul, and that everyone has the sensitivity to recognize that soul. Being surrounded by objects is like being in a train station during rush hour: sometimes it is nicer just being quietly alone.

We all rely heavily on communications. We live in a realm of disturbances that impair our vision and our perception. Too many things talk to us at the same time.

We naturally tend to deal with these by arranging them into agreeable compositions — rather like making music. We coordinate our clothes, our foods and our homes.

An alternative approach is clearly to focus, to embrace essence — a case of stepping

back and allowing ourselves the moment to sense the soul.

By removing the noise that surrounds us, we acknowledge from within the beauty of what remains. Think of nature in the early hours. The divine simplicity of mornings – a single bird whose song drifts out to us from a dense mist.

## truth and freedom

A place becomes your home when you become sincere. Then the home is where truth and freedom are to be found. You can dress to protect and project an image you think is worthy of you. I do not think, however, that creating your home is about asserting an image. Not even your private image for yourself.

You can live a life on two or more planes – with a public face and a private one, a reception room and a locked bedroom. I believe neither is entirely satisfactory.

A place becomes a home when the guiding and arranging hand is neither private nor public. A home is not a mirror of your image nor an environment to cultivate this image.

A home is not about image at all, it is about a you that does not require an image.

# prelude

ROOTS OF ZEN. SPIRIT OF ZEN. ZEN ESSENTIALS.
PURITY AND SIMPLICITY. STILLNESS AND
FLUIDITY. ORNAMENT AND FUNCTION.
MINDFULNESS. LIGHT, SPACE AND SOLIDITY.
ARTLESSNESS AND ARTISTRY. THE CURVE OF
A GOOD ACTION. TRUTH AND PERCEPTION.
CEREMONY.

"Before a person knows Zen, a chair is
a chair and a stone a stone. After a first
glimpse of the truth of Zen, a chair is
no longer a chair and a stone no longer
a stone. After enlightenment, a chair is
once more a chair and a stone once
more a stone."

– Zen saying, adapted

# roots of zen

Zen is a tradition of Buddhist teachings and practices that originated in China (as *ch'an*) and later became characteristic of Japan. In the ninth century CE Zen teachers in China began to forge a new teaching style, based on the interpretation of paradoxical stories, which came to be known in Japan as *koans*. Typically, a novice might be expected to focus his mind on a knotty intellectual conundrum – for example, the word *mu* ("nothingness") – until an awakening occurred.

Japanese monks began to import such Chinese teachings into their home country from around 1000CE, notably Dogen (1200–1253), who established the famous Soto Zen school, which emphasized the importance of *zazen*, or seated meditation, by which enlightenment would come gradually. In contrast to this school was Rinzai Zen, which claimed that enlightenment (*satori*) could dawn suddenly, in a flash of insight, thanks to the mind-opening power of the koan.

In Zen, an enlightened state of mind is seen as a source of profound peace. To attain this happy state, we need to unlearn bad habits and emotions. The awakened mind is an empty mirror that reflects everything perfectly and responds to everything appropriately.

Over the centuries, native Japanese culture and Zen have blended to create an astonishing variety of art forms – including archery, flower arrangement, gardening, poetry, calligraphy and the tea ceremony. All have in common a concentration on the moment, a stripping away of inessentials. To these specific arts might be added a modern Western variant – the art of living well, in a calm, harmonious, beautiful environment.

# spirit of zen

In its emphasis on simplicity, purity and naturalness, Zen offers an antidote to all that is excessively formal, pompous or contrived. In its feeling for the essence of things – a kind of anti-intellectualism – it offers a philosophical alternative to traditional Western belief systems that may seem increasingly remote from the way it feels to live now, in the modern age.

But what about Zen as an approach to the home – the way we organize and decorate our rooms, design and plant our gardens, prepare and cook our meals? In fact, Zen can serve as a valuable and time-honoured compass in these areas, a set of principles by which we can make our decisions.

Is this to trivialize Zen, to shrink it down to a repertoire of fashionable style rules? Not at all. Cooking, sleeping, eating, gardening, meditating are all charged with special importance in Zen, which recognizes that our surroundings contribute to and reflect our peace of mind. Few would wish to re-create a Zen monastery in all its austerity. Yet by taking a more contemplative and purist attitude to our home, we can all learn that style is not something we put on like new clothes: at its most worthwhile, it can bring us quiet atmospheric satisfactions, the sense of the home being just right for us, a tranquil place where we can find profound and lasting contentment.

This book looks at three main areas in which Zen can make a difference in our lives — the home, the garden, and cookery — without our having to subscribe to esoteric beliefs. Here and there are starbursts of Zen wisdom, to set a mood, or provoke a teasing or poetic thought. But the main messages of the book lie in its pictures — look and be enlightened.

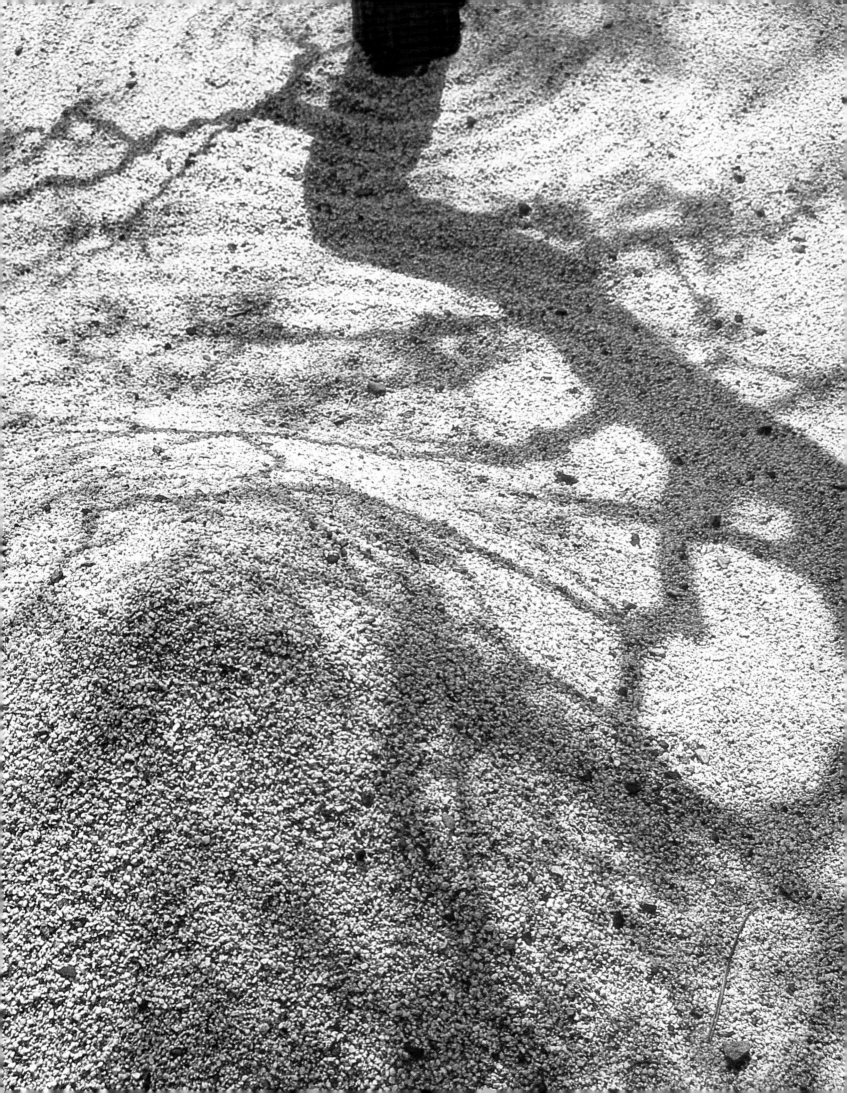

# zen essentials

## purity and simplicity

Zen believes in the thing itself — the world stripped down to its bare bones. This is very much a matter of grasping the self-evident reality of objects. A stone is a stone, a tree a tree. We can easily say this but we do not fully understand what we are saying until we weigh the stone in our hands and feel its coldness against our cheek, or run our fingers over the trunk and branches of the tree and feel the flakes of bark crumbling as we do so. Words do not help us to get closer to the truth: on the contrary, they distance us from the truth.

In design terms, such a philosophy will obviously value the purity of natural materials, used nakedly. Zen relishes the grain of wood, the weave of matting, the roughness of unpolished rock. However, because there is no real division between the external and the internal worlds, Zen also finds beauty in the the perfection of the man-made artifact. Neither natural nor artificial beauty is superior, and Zen's ultimate aim is often an attempt to blend the two. The Zen rock garden, for example, manipulates nature to a high level of abstraction — the idea being to imitate nature's inner essence, not its outward form.

Advocates of Zen strive to rid themselves of clutter, as this too brings them to a kind of purity. In part this is a rejection of acquisitiveness. Some might even say that it's better to have a lump of granite on your coffee table than a Fabergé jewelbox. There is a touch of austerity or even self-denial in such preferences. In the modern home this tends to be manifested more as understatement and effective use of space than as actual deprivation or discomfort.

stillness and fluidity

A typical view in an authentic Zen garden is of a weathered rock standing amid the swirling furrows of raked gravel, like a stack of granite emerging from the sea. The implied contrast of stillness and fluidity is a key Zen concept. Stillness is important, because unless the mind is still, it cannot find peace. Yet the world itself is endlessly changing, flowing around us in its endlessly busy chance events. The spirit at the heart of all this restlessness remains motionless, partaking of infinity. An indoor equivalent of the rock in the sea or stream might be an antique Buddha statue, catching the changing light as the day progresses from dawn to dusk. Just as water and light flow, so too does space itself. And in Zen interiors we are often aware of space as a broad, shallow river, flowing gracefully around the furniture. Circulation routes, like much else in Zen, seem natural and inevitable.

## ornament and function

Ornament in the Western sense has no place in the Zen tradition, because it comes from the shallow, prettifying part of our minds — the part that sees nature and presumptuously seeks to improve upon it, or to rival it. To be genuinely artistic is to create not a rival to nature but an homage to nature. If we display the grain of timber on an expanse of floor, this is an act of reverence for the characteristics of trees. If we hang a landscape painting on our wall, it will be one that catches the essence of a scene in deft, intuitive strokes, not one that dazzles us with the realism of foliage meticulously painted leaf by leaf.

To display, for example, a seashell in an alcove, is to acknowledge the inexpressible profundity of the sea and its creatures. To display, instead, a lump of driftwood is to recognize and accept the beautiful erosions and witherings of time. (Japan, of course, is an island nation, with strong maritime traditions, and references to the sea would be perfectly apt in a Zen-style interior.)

These are objects of nature. But what about the Zen impulse to display a galvanized bucket in a kitchen? – or to appreciate, say, an old-fashioned bathtub standing in the middle of a bathroom? What is appealed to here is the nobility of function. Work, however mundane or repetitive, has great value in the Zen view of life, and so implements of work, designed to serve their function well, acquire a special dignity. Transparency is also valued. And so something like a garden rake, or a showerhead, has the positive quality of openly admitting its own function. Esthetics has an ethical dimension. Work, honesty and effective design merge into a good reason for putting functional objects on display.

## mindfulness

Zen composes in three dimensions: it recognizes the observer who moves from one viewpoint to the next, in a garden or a room, having a succession of planned experiences. These might be a series of views, perhaps (in gardens) even vistas with a painterly quality. But above all Zen design anticipates an observer who will

be fully alert to all aspects of the scene. The quality of noticing details, without distraction from ambitions or anxieties, is known as "mindfulness". Mindful people pay full attention to all that the senses convey. Hence the importance of detail. Every square inch of a room or garden, like every precious moment of our lives, deserves to be honoured.

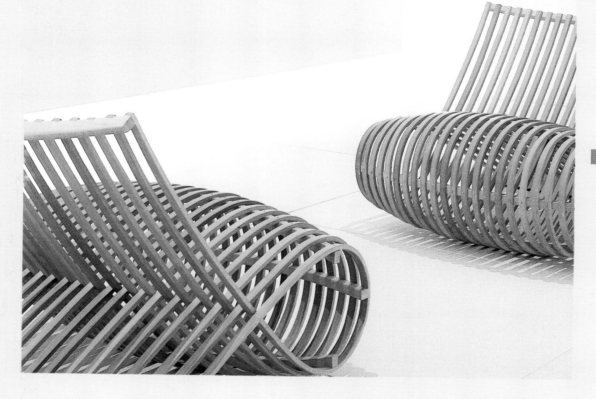

Space and solidity are the framework in which light flows wherever it can. Like water finding its own level, light travels to the very limits of possibility — whatever is beyond its reach is either solid or shadow. These three ingredients are the basic elements of spatial design. Notice in the chair above how light (or space) has a presence that is equal to the solid wood.

**ight, space and solidity**

And, similarly, look how a narrow diagonal of light, in the attic bedroom above, is strong enough to balance a whole expanse of shadow – rather in the way that a clump of bent reeds might balance the lake to which they form an edge. Light and shadow bring out the poetry of form, like the folds in a kimono that reveal the hidden postures of the body.

## artlessness and artistry

The emphasis on simplicity makes Zen design or art seem surprisingly modern to the Western eye. Lines are clean, pattern is minimal, colour is used with restraint. These are certainly characteristic features, yet somehow they do not account for what is really special about Zen – any more than an inventory of bones, muscles and organs tells us what is special about human beings.

The missing factor can perhaps be defined as an intuitive flair for creating just the right effect. A Zen artist displays an inner confidence and sureness of purpose, so that the design or artifact created looks and feels somehow inevitable. Artistry is applied, and in a very disciplined way, often following an elaborate set of rules. But the resulting creation seems to spring mysteriously from within, from the spirit. The effect is one of effortlessness, a work created without inter-ference from the critical faculties of the mind.

All this is seen clearly in the use of the curve in a Zen home or garden – for example, the curved edging to a path, or the overall sweeping shape of a flower arrangement. Zen curves have an asymmetric grace – and even where they have been made following rigorous principles of geometry, they look like sudden and spontaneous gestures of the mind.

This instinctive "rightness" comes over in the choice of colours or shades, the arrange-ment of furniture, the grouping of objects in a still life, or the planting in a garden. And just as there is an inevitability about the individual parts, so too there is a sense of harmonious perfection in the overall impact of a room or outdoor space. Anyone in tune with Zen will feel inspired to bring into being the beautiful creations their inner harmony facilitates.

the curve of

# a good action

A curve is the achievement of purpose and the relaxation of effort after a good action is performed.

## truth and perception

As we have seen, Zen sees value in things as they are – in the words of the American poet Wallace Stevens, "a tune beyond us, yet ourselves". The minutiae of phenomena are experienced in a spirit of mindfulness – that is, directly and attentively, not filtered through the distorting veil of the ego's daydreaming insecurities. So this is a culture, we might be led to conclude, that opts for naturalness instead of artifice, truth instead of disguise? Not quite. In fact, Zen creativity often concentrates on achieving particular effects, capturing an essential beauty through elaborate, carefully controlled contrivance.

We have only to think of the Zen garden to savour to the full the underlying paradox – that profound truths are revealed through strategies of imitation or disguise. Imitation is apparent in the idea that raked gravel represents the sea, that a flat rock might represent a terrapin, a scattering of differently sized rocks a samurai and his sons. Disguise is apparent in the way in which the boundaries of a garden are skillfully hidden to give the illusion of infinite space – scarcely ever are we presented with an endstopped view leading the eye to a wall or fence, as we are in many Western gardens.

Even elements not directly imitative tend to have symbolic layers of meaning, so that we cannot look at, for example, a pine tree and see it as just a pine tree. Its symbolic associations of human longevity (also, courage, resolution, good fortune and, more specifically, the strength to ignore unjust criticism), require us to treat it with special respect. It is one of the many paradoxes of Zen that a stone is a stone is a stone, while at the same time being so much more.

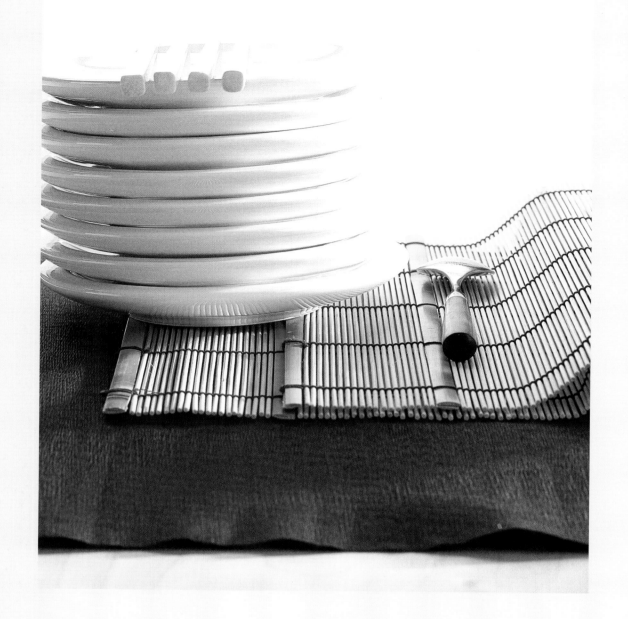

### ceremony

A nobleman was invited by an artisan to come to his house in the suburbs of Tokyo, for a tea ceremony. The setting and utensils were all extremely humble. Everything was laid out with refined though simple dignity. The two met and conversed in a friendly manner. Then the nobleman bowed to the artisan, and

together they drank their tea. The significance of such a meeting is that both men shared the Way. This idea is almost impossible to put into words – Zen, remember, mistrusts words as a vehicle for truth. Any meal, snack or tea-drinking session conducted in a spirit of attentiveness and generosity, without pretension, has the capacity to be a profound experience.

# nature

THE FLOWER OF BEING. SECLUSION AND SPACE.
WATER AND MOUNTAINS IN GRAVEL. STONE AND
ROCK. BAMBOO. THE SNAKE AND THE BOW.
BAREFOOT ON WOOD. THE GARDEN'S EYE.
WALKING OVER WATER. SOUNDSCAPES.
THE PATIENCE OF TIME. BLOSSOM. THE FAMILY
OF GREEN. LIVING FLAME. THE WISDOM
OF LEAVES.

"The garden promises
all nature's infinite virtue,
just an arm's length away."
                — *Modern Japanese haiku*

The Zen garden summarizes an important discovery we have made about our own place within nature. This makes it profound, as well as beautiful. Far from being merely a place of recreation, or a green bath in which to soothe tired eyes, the garden has deep connections with the spirit. It is movingly symbolic of the human quest for self-understanding – a place for meditation and simple contentment.

A Zen garden is the perfect union of nature and contrivance. Its subtle combinations of just a few elements, within a colour palette largely restricted to foliage shades and the pinks and whites of fruit blossom, provides an inspiring antidote to the riotous colour and obsessive symmetry of many Western gardens. A Japanese gardener might see the beauty of the flowers used in a Gertrude Jekyll-style English country border – but would question why such beautiful things must be spoiled by blending them together so that their individuality is lost.

In the Japanese garden we are acutely aware of the special characteristics of plants and objects. This is partly because of their strangeness – think of the tonsured trees, or the quirkiness of a large rock placed within a sea of raked sand or gravel. But it is also partly because the individual components of the garden are so harmoniously arranged – and so well maintained.

Any garden plot can acquire Zen characteristics through careful choice of planting, rock, gravel and water features, and more explicit references in the form of oriental-style statuary and ornament. The more obvious cultural signposts, such as the clichéd Japanese lantern or *stupa* (stone tower), are probably best avoided, unless they are patently or convincingly genuine rather than obviously mass produced. Paths will be winding, creating a series of surprises as one strolls around the plot. Boundaries will be disguised to give the illusion of endless space — the "borrowed garden" effect known as *shakkei*. Pebbles and moss banks will add to the ambience, and some of the shrubs might be closely cropped in green mounds. Evergreens and rocks will make a hard frame for the garden, with other planting treated as infilling, or providing seasonal effects within the permanent skeleton — blossoming of cherries, joyful flowering of azaleas, irises showing their colours at the pondside, maple leaves smouldering as the year begins to fall away, the blooming of magnolia and plum acting as a glorious bridge between winter and spring.

The overall composition will have clarity and confidence — suggesting the visionary hand of an artist rather than the piecemeal accumulation of impulse decisions (or impulse buys in the store or garden centre). Indeed, Japanese gardens were greatly inspired by Chinese landscape painting, with pine trees pruned to copy painted tree shapes precisely.

In gardens that lack water (ponds are troublesome to maintain but worthwhile for the tranquility they bring), you might consider simulating waves and ripples in gravel or even sand – as in the famous "dry water" gardens of Japan. The basic idea is to imitate, with deft strokes of the rake, the way in which water eddies around rocks and islands – represented in the garden in miniature form.

A less well-known feature of Japanese gardening is the pleasure taken in finding a new use for old objects. A modern version of this might be to site, say, an old millstone in a bed of gravel, or to edge a border using broken roof tiles.

# the flower of being

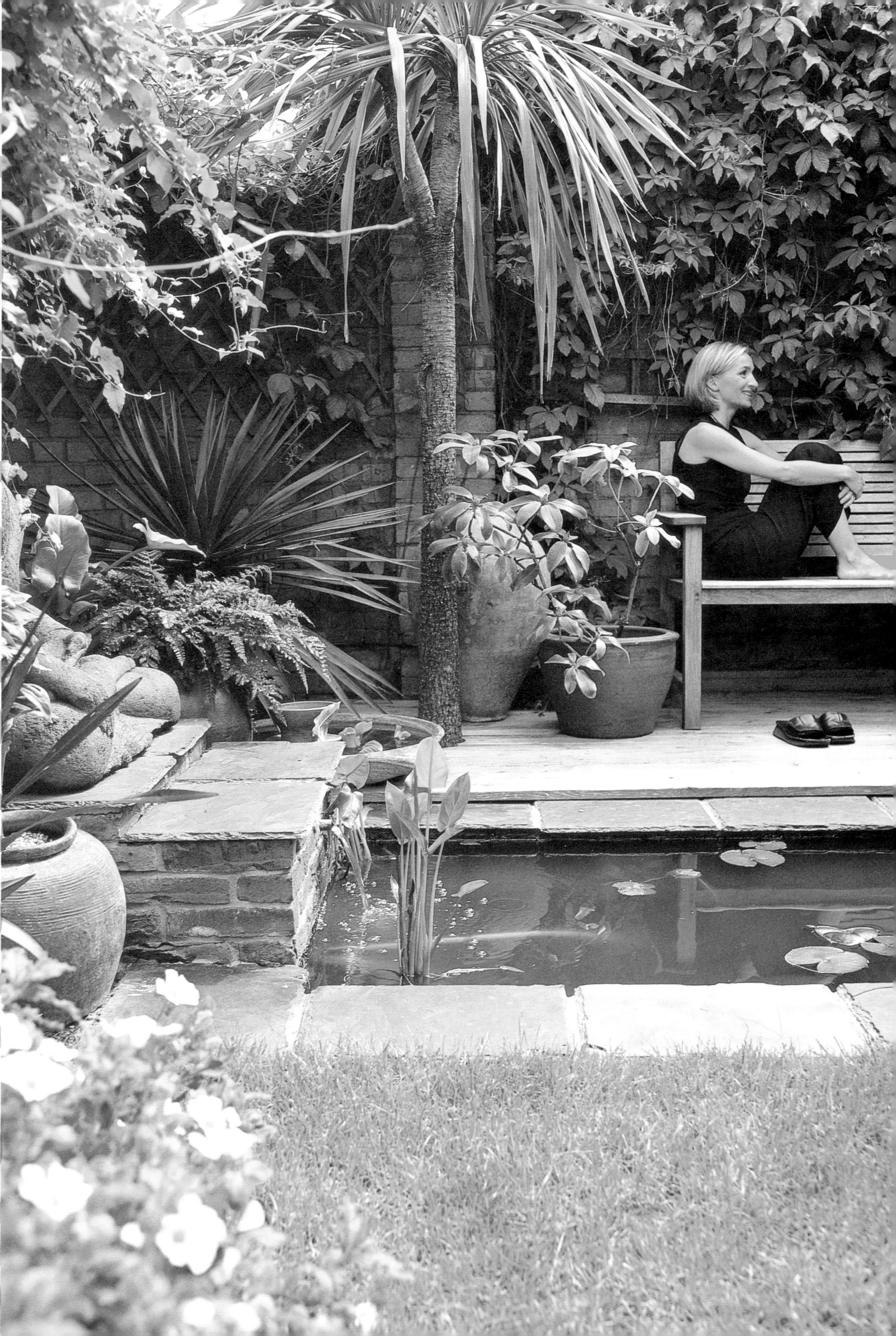

The Zen garden is quintessentially a place for meditation. It is a three-dimensional reflection of the inner landscape of the settled mind. Strolling around this idealized place, deciding which path to follow only at the last moment, taking the time to savour sights, sounds and scents, creates a refined enjoyment of the senses, while at the same time offering a leisurely opportunity for the gentle meditative play of our spirit upon nature. Alternatively, you might choose to meditate while seated. Find a tranquil site and sit comfortably, your hands loosely clasped – use a soft cushion if you like. Take long, slow, deep breaths, concentrating all your attention on the in-breath and out-breath, until you feel relaxed. Then begin to let the sights and sounds of the garden drift through your consciousness. Do not cling to any thoughts or perceptions: just let them float in and out of awareness like blossom on a light spring breeze.

Light filtered through leaves is just one way to experience seclusion. In a shady clearing like this, with tantalizing pathways leading off, you can sit and listen to the sounds both within and outside the garden. As the sense of peace accumulates, cares dissolve into nothingness. Here, even the boundary fence lets in light, so that you feel enclosed but not contained.

# seclusion and

# space

"The almighty sky does not hinder
white clouds in their flight."
— *Sen nu Ryokan*

# water and mountains in gravel

Zen sensibility finds one of its clearest expressions in the gravel-and-rock "dry garden", or *karesansui* – an abstract composition of raked gravel (or sand) and rocks, in which these components symbolize water and mountains. Such a garden exemplifies the idea of *yugen* – meaning profound suggestiveness, the creation of a work of art with just a few carefully selected elements that move the onlooker's spirit, without any recourse to prettiness or embellishment. The curving raked lines of the *karesansui*, silted with changing shadows as the sun moves across the sky, fill the meditative mind with peace.

Gravel is easier to discipline than sand: use a homemade coarse wooden rake to shape and maintain your patterns. Where bright sun is likely to reach the area, avoid white sand, which can look glaring. To prevent weeds peeking through, place a tough sheet of plastic, cut to size, on top of the earth, and lay the gravel thickly over the plastic. Two possible patterns are shown here; the conical mound of gravel is intended to represent Mount Fuji, which has sacred associations.

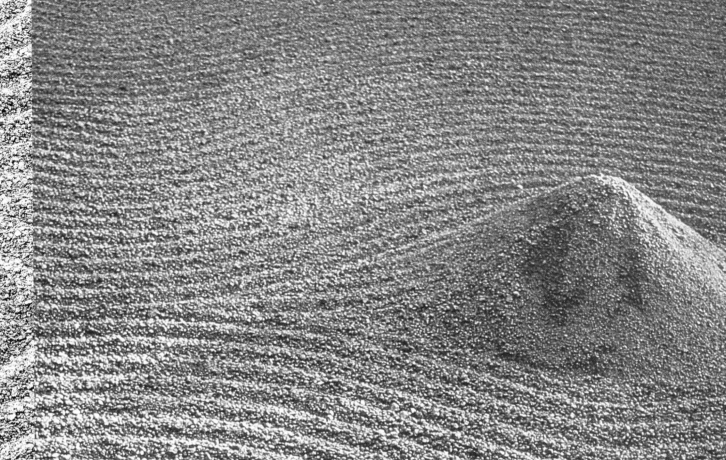

# stone and rock

Few features of the garden have such strong character as a large stone or rock, alone or in a group. Our imagination is easily persuaded that a pile of stones is a formidable mountain range – in the same way that a statue is imbued with human attributes. This miniaturism is a feature of the Zen garden, yet the aim was originally not to imitate nature directly, but to imitate the effects familiar from Chinese landscape ink painting – a representation of a representation. At the same time, a distinctive rock is perceived as a focus of energy – the vital breath, or *ki*, that permeates nature. When positioning rocks

"Even though the mountain becomes the sea, words cannot open another's mind."
– *Mu mon*

in the garden, the Japanese often think of them as animate – perhaps a turtle (if the rock is flattish) or a crane or wise old man (if more upright). Some rock arrangements symbolize episodes from myth. An arrangement of stones with moss around them are regarded as particularly harmonious, the stones having *yang* or masculine energy, the moss having its *yin* or feminine counterpart. Occasionally, a volcano would be re-created in the garden, as in the view opposite, a reference to the elemental forces that loom large over our lives.

"In the pasture of this world, I endlessly push aside the tall grasses in search of the bull." – *Kakuan*

Bamboo, a woody-stemmed grass, has poetic associations in Japan. The bamboo, the pine and the plum are the Three Friends of Winter – a triad of good omens. The bamboo's straight stem striving toward the heavens – bamboo is the fastest-growing of all the world's plants – symbolizes the purposefulness of meditation; while the hollowness within suggests the unburdened spirit. Tough and practical, this material is also water-resistant enough to be used in kitchens and bathrooms, or for channelling water in the garden. Bamboo fencing, plaited in regular patterns, is a minor art form. There are many species of bamboo available to gardeners, of varying heights and degrees of hardiness (the most common hardy types reach up to 15 feet/4 metres). A clump makes a fine windbreak, and will send out relaxing rustling sounds as it sways in the breeze – for some Daoist masters the rustle of bamboo was the symbol of enlightenment.

"Late into the night, I know the snow must be deep now –
from time to time I hear the cracking of bamboos."
                                        – Bai juyi

# bamboo

"Unfettered at last, a travelling monk,
I pass the old Zen barrier."

– *Manan*

# the snake and the bow

There are two types of curve to which we respond at a deep level – sinuous and shallow. Look for existing ones in your garden and draw attention to them by giving emphasis to the edging. A shadow formed by a slight change of level alongside the path, as in the picture at left, will underscore the curve and heighten its beauty. You might want to modify a straight line to a bow, or a bow to a snake; the whole mood of a garden can be changed by such gestures. Although considerable labour may be involved, the reward will be a greater sense of space, of neverendingness, compared with the finite space suggested by an endstopped path of straight lines. In the second example to the right we see how paving stones within a garden corridor can create a gently curving path *without* such re-landscaping.

A snake knows the earth much better than we,
two legs above its level.
A bow knows better than the archer
how to send an arrow faster than the archer's
thought.

"The mind can go in a thousand directions.
 But on this lovely path, I walk in peace.
 With each step, a gentle wind blows.
 With each step, a flower blooms."
— *Mu mon*

# barefoot on wood

Wood decking, of course, is not a material found in the traditional Japanese garden. Yet slatted timber walkways and seating areas often fit well into a Zen-style setting. The parallel lines of individual slats suggest the infinite, and therefore the spiritual. Arranged diagonally, the slats can make meditative patterns. The contrast between decking and boulders or stones near by is particularly effective. Underfoot, decking feels pleasantly yielding — making this the ideal flooring material for barefoot enjoyment of your garden, provided that the wood has been sanded to eliminate splinters. Soften the edges visually with strategically placed containers, or with ferns or other foliage overlapping onto the timber surface. One word of warning: decking in damp climates can be a slippery and dangerous disaster, and rotting will soon remind you of the indomitable vigour of nature. In high-rainfall areas, however, consider using decking to floor a covered gallery or, if exposed, in a sun-trap where the sun has the best chance of drying it out.

# the garden's eye

Think of a pond as the eye of the garden – gathering the changing sky in its gaze. The classic Japanese garden was epitomized as *chisen kaiyu teien*, or "pond-spring-strolling garden" – that is, a garden with a spring-fed pond. Ponds are a superb addition to the atmosphere of a garden, and through careful choice of edging, planting and fishlife can create a wonderfully Japanese effect. The impression to strive for is of mysterious black depths (use a black pond-liner), waterlilies, and fish that swim tantalizingly in and out of view. Waterlily clumps would be thought of in Japan as islands in a vast sea.

"Old pond,
    a moment of leap and splash –
    look, a frog!"
        – *Basho*

To achieve the ideal, there are many practical considerations to bear in mind, and no one should embark upon pondmaking without researching thoroughly the whole question of siting, installation and maintenance. For example, however attractive the notion of a foliage-shaded pond, one must remember that shade inhibits plant growth, and to clear the water of fallen leaves in autumn can be a major chore. A good choice of waterlily for a shallow pond would be the red 'Purpurata' or pure white 'Alba', while for deeper waters try the *Nymphaea marliacea* 'Chromatella' whose soft, yellow flowers look stunning on dark water.

"Follow the stream, have faith in its course. It will go on its own way, meandering here, trickling there. It will find the grooves, the cracks, the crevices. Just follow it. Never let it out of your sight."

— *Sheng yen*

# walking over water

It is always a privilege to be able to cross water. We lose our routine contact with solid ground and inhabit a more mysterious element. In the garden this encounter may last only a few seconds, but it is worth investing some imagination in designing such crossings as a special experience. A zigzag arrangement makes stepping-stones more eyecatching. Three contrasting approaches are shown here. At left is the checkerboard approach, in which the quartering of the pavestones is echoed by the larger pattern made by water, stone and low hedging. Above left, the route across water is heralded by a "moon arch" set within a wall. And in the third example (above right) zigzag decking calls to mind the Eastern belief that evil spirits could travel only in a straight line: in attempting such a walkway, they would fall into the water and drown!

# soundscapes

Gravity moves water, wind moves leaves, or grasses. The sounds they make are refreshment for the troubled soul. Place garden seating where you will benefit most from such natural sound effects. Create simple sounds with a wind chime – for example, a bamboo mobile jangling softly to produce the effect of an aural rainbow. A typically Japanese device is the *shishi-odoshi*, or deer-scarer. This is a hinged bamboo trough that fills with water from a little stream, that clacks down onto another piece of bamboo once the water reaches critical mass. Though abrupt, the clacking of the deer-scarer at fixed intervals can be curiously soothing. Always remember, the most tranquil sounds will be birdsong: make sure there is plenty of winter food for garden birds, and a nestbox or two in the breeding season. Sounds are as important as sights or smells: after all, the best cooks know when rice is cooked from the sound it makes, not from lifting the lid of the pan.

Go into the garden and listen to the silences between the sounds: this is the real music of nature.

"An instant of realization sees endless time.
Endless time is as one moment.
When you comprehend the endless moment,
you realize the person who is seeing it."

— *Mu mon*

# the patience of time

Central to Zen Buddhism is the practice of *zazen*, or "just sitting" — the human experience of the patience of time. Create the sense of time in your garden by welcoming the arrival of moss, ivy or lichen — let these plants become symbols of ancient sages, bringing truth to your garden. Similarly, meditate on the flat-topped bole of a sawn tree — each concentric circle represents the turn of another year. Let this be your mandala for quiet meditation.

The rings of a tree-trunk:
ourselves reflected back to infancy
in two mirrors,
one opposite the other.

The enlightened mind finds the Lotus Paradise everywhere. For lesser mortals, it is found in the tranquility of the garden. In some Zen gardens cherry and plum groves create a magical seasonal effect. The Japanese lunar calendar has plum in the first month, cherry in the second. Both are rich in symbolism. In China (from which Zen derives much of its spirit) the plum is a symbol of immortality, while in Japan it is one of the three trees of good omen, a "friend of winter", announcing the New Year. The flowering cherry (which bears no fruit) is a symbol of purity. It is also associated in Japan with good fortune, especially in the marriage ceremony, when cherry-blossom tea is drunk. Cherry blossom prefigures the flowering of rice, and the abundance and longevity of its blossom in any one year is held to predict the quality of the rice harvest. Both trees offer a fine way to evoke the essence of Zen in a modern garden.

# blossom

"If someone asked me to define
the spirit of Japan, I would call it
the blossom of the mountain cherry,
scattering its fragrance in
the morning sun."
    – Motoori Norinaga

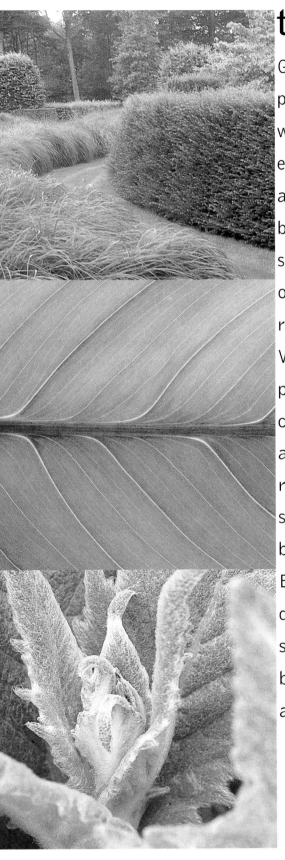

# the family of green

Green is the colour of awakening, of hope, and of the processes of life itself. In China, green corresponds with the trigram *ch'en*, meaning "arousing" – a reference to the welcome upheavals of spring. This is also the hue of immortality, symbolized by the green bough – after all, green re-emerges from winter snows every year without fail. We cannot see shades of green without at the same time seeing textures: the range of both in our garden flora is virtually infinite. Within the permanent framework of green, made partly of evergreen trees and shrubs (sometimes close-cropped into tight mounds, or *kari-komi*) but also partly of moss and even the patina of lichen on rocks, the Japanese revel in the changes of the seasons. The coming of cherry blossom in spring is celebrated in special viewing parties, when *sake* is drunk. But even more subtle transitions are savoured with delicate connoiseurship – for example, the moment in spring when bright green leaves of maple start to break from their buds, and the grasses turning paler as they dry.

# living flame

As autumn's rusty
wheel turns,
even the maple leaves
give out their cry of
exultation.

Summer in the Japanese garden gives us lovely flowers of wisteria, iris and azaleas, as well as brilliant blue bellflowers – one of the few flowering plants the Japanese favour in massed clumps. The fragrant gardenia and the lotus, with its Buddhist associations, are also typical. Chrysanthemum anticipates winter. For foliage, autumn's glories are the flame-red foliage colours of Japanese maple, *Acer palmatum*, available in many different cultivars. A single specimen of this, or as an alternative something like *Cotinus coggygria*, the smoke bush, makes a dramatic climax to a stroll among garden greenery.

# the wisdom of leaves

A single ruddy leaf on the black surface of a pond: appreciate such details — they are as crucial to the experience of a garden as more contrived effects. Meditate on the branching veins of leaves as well as on their colouring. Focus mindfully on the task when clearing away fallen leaves in autumn. Far from being mundane, this action is the symbolic sweeping away of the old to make way, after the hiatus of winter, for the new life of spring.

"The body is the tree of wisdom,
the mind a bright mirror in its stand."
— *Shen hsui*

As leaves break free from their trees, they are like the flip of the date on a million electronic calendars, or the turning of pages in all the world's libraries.

# living

EAST–WEST FUSION. ASYMMETRY. DIMENSIONS
OF ZEN. SCREENS. THE FIRE AT THE HEART OF
THE HOME. A SCENTED HEARTH. THE ALL-
PURPOSE ROOM. THE ZEN WORKSPACE.
A WATERFALL OF STEPS AND STAIRS. FACING
ALL WAYS. ANGLES AND ABSTRACTIONS.
BLACK AND WHITE. YELLOW. A SENSE OF TWO
WORLDS. JAPANESE BOXES. ALCOVES. TABLE-
TOP NATURE. CHARACTER IN PLANTS. OUTSIDE
INSIDE. PONDS AND ROCKS INDOORS.

"Each moment outshines the one before.
Whatever happens, this is the present.
Make your home here."
— *Modern Zen meditation*

A traditional Japanese house is cool in winter and warm in summer — a reflection of the world outside. Furniture is minimal, and there are no chairs. To a follower of Zen, such austerity would be seen not as deprivation but as succour for the inner self. In the modern Western home, few would want to relinquish traditional notions of comfort. Yet there are many ways to be true to Zen principles even within the context of a Western lifestyle. Most crucially, in assimilating Zen into our daily lives, we learn to banish clutter, over-decoration, self-importance and excessive nostalgia — both in our surroundings and in the way we use them.

In the Zen-style living room, furniture is simple and artlessly placed. Objects used decoratively are chosen not for a display of wealth or taste, but for their intrinsic characteristics — we have to feel that they are interesting in themselves, and not merely as aspects of our own esthetic sensibilities.

The Western reflex is to straighten, to polish, to smooth, to bedeck – and to arrange with unnatural symmetry. Zen, however, does not shy away from irregularity, roughness, bareness. To bring some natural thing – a piece of driftwood or a ragged lump of quartz – into the home is to observe reverence toward the world beyond ourselves. If instead you choose to display an artifact – for example, an old wooden Buddha picked up on travels in Asia, or in a local fleamarket – what does it matter if time has warped or cracked the artifact in places? Such imperfections only add to the object's uniqueness, to its relationship with the rest of the world.

Close to the heart of Zen is an esthetic characterized by the word *miyabi*. This was used to indicate those aspects of beauty that only a highly refined sensitivity could appreciate: pale colours, fragile petals, the textures of various papers. This is in part the appreciation of gesture — a stroke of the calligrapher's brush, a branch arranged with subtle effect in a vase. When we respond to such nuances, we are responding to the transience of material things — and, consequently, to a profound spiritual reality.

The main goal of pure Zen architecture is openness accompanied by lightness and flexibility. Structure is exposed to the eye, walls are sliding paper partitions, or *fusuma*. As there are no chairs, eye level is much lower than in a Western home. Rooms are lit by *fusuma shoji*, or softly shaded lanterns, made of a flat white paper so strong that you cannot tear it with your hands. Visitors enter through a doorway where they remove their shoes, and then passes through a bare wood-floored hallway to enter a living room as empty as a monastic cell. Often, the only furniture will be a small central table around which the guests sit on square cushions. A *tokonoma,* or picture recess, may contain an illustrated scroll on which Zen calligraphy is displayed – presented as a meditation in its own right, with straight lines representing oneness and circles signifying emptiness.

The modern Zen-style living room, taking this purist ideal as a starting point, may branch off in any number of different directions. Yet the outcome, if the Zen spirit is not to be too much dissolved, will always have certain ingredients – a reverence for texture, natural light as a permanent house guest, and in some not necessarily describable way a profound sense of *openness* in the planning and choice of contents which reflects the owners' open minds and hearts.

# east–west fusion

The marriage of East and West has become possibly the most significant theme in interior design at the turn of the twenty-first century. This reflects the opening of the East to travellers, and a yearning for something more spiritual and more mysterious in our lives. But how well do Eastern and Western styles fuse? The answer is that the mix can be very appealing provided that the Western ingredients are handled with intuitive sensitivity and understatement. Natural arrangements of plants and flowers help the chemistry, as does the avoidance

of too much busy pattern. Think of a room containing an elaborate Eastern carving, such as the Buddha here. Substitute for this carving a modern sculpture of, say, a horse, or a Baroquely-carved abstract piece. The overall esthetic effect could well be very similar. Eastern and Western artifacts can sometimes be interchangeable — what is important is how they are used within their setting. Here the generously-upholstered chairs, with their debt to European eighteenth-century styling, present a dynamic contrast with the Buddha; their whiteness helps to unify the disparate elements of the room.

Asymmetry is Zen because it does not revere the rules of artificial balance. Two urns, positioned one at either side of a fireplace, need not be equidistant from the centre. Look at the positioning of the urns, arum lilies and picture in the photograph opposite, a mixture of precise alignments and asymmetrical arrangements that feels instinctively right in a flash of conviction – the "diamond thunderbolt". Trust your own mind's capacity for recognizing this flash when it comes.

Asymmetry is Zen
Balance is Zen
Asymmetrical balance is Zen
Symmetrical balance is rigidity

"In this house of meditation we realize that everything is void.
In this temple of debate we analyze nuances of truth."

– *Xie Lingyun*

# dimensions of Zen

Some rooms, in the fascination of their floor surface or covering, and the positioning of sculptural objects, might be seen as the indoor equivalents of the Zen garden with its raked gravel and craggy rocks. A typically Zen-style floor is one that is rich in the grain of natural wood, although a more authentically Japanese approach might be to use matting. In the larger picture here, note the alcove with its low table and floor cushions — evoking the tea ceremony at its height of purism. Low seating, seen left and top, greatly increases the sense of a room being amply sized in relation to the scale of its occupants.

# screens

Where in a Western room there would normally be a wall, a Japanese home would have a screen, giving more flexibility in the use of space. There are sliding paper-skinned doors (*fusuma*) and also paper-covered interior screens which may be either structural (*shoji*) or freestanding (*suitate* and *boyobu*). Panels in screens may be infilled with bamboo matting or closely-spaced reeds, instead of paper. In a Western setting you might consider using a screen to create a Zen-like atmosphere, to provide privacy or to create an area for dining. An effective strategy can be to frame a conventional window with paper screens, off-setting the garden with a touch of rectilinear design. The shadows of leaves falling on paper are a typically Japanese way to appreciate trees around the house.

Opening a door in the conventional Western way, by turning a handle and then pulling it toward you, is an action that has no place in the Eastern tradition. More typical is the sliding screen or partition. There are endless Western variations on this theme. The action of sliding is more graceful than opening a hinged door: it reveals the view into the next space without interference from the architecture.

Pull the door toward you or push it away —
the next room hits you on the head.
Slide the door and you are a magician, conjuring
the next room from endless possibility.

# the fire at the heart of the home

Fire dances forth from fuel in an almost mystical transfiguration. We are transfixed by the flames, which serve as a flickering focus for our thoughts. Heighten this sense of focus by an appropriate arrangement of furniture. The use of a rough-hewn log as a side table (below) evokes the chopping of firewood – giving us a Zen-like reminder of the work that makes comfort possible. On a miniature scale the vitality of fire can be echoed in candles. Use accents of red fabric nearby (as in the detail, left) to amplify the glow.

"Put your hands up, palms outward, to feel the warmth of chrysanthemums."

– *Modern haiku*

All life is like a phoenix, re-creating itself
again and again from its own ashes.

White throws in an all-white room: in such a setting scented logs piled in a hearth really do evoke warmth in winter, a comforting blaze in a world of snow. Fire is the element of reason, expressiveness and good manners. Wherever there is fire, there is vitality – another presence that is almost human. Bear in mind that different woods have different smells – see if you can get to know them. You might also put herbs on the logs to release their aromas.

# a scented hearth

# the all-purpose room

The combined living space – with living room, dining room and kitchen all between the same walls – has many practical advantages, as well as being thoroughly Zen in its spatial versatility. Light flows freely, favouring all parts of the room with its gifts. There is a tremendous sense of space, which has the effect of lightening the spirit. And it is easier for the cook to be hospitable to guests. Here, one steps down from the kitchen into an L-shaped area for dining and relaxing. The theme of fluidity is continued in the open staircase.

"Calm, activity – each has its uses."
– Soan

# the zen workspace

Zen simplicity in a study or home office is not only esthetic but can also serve a practical function. Purified, your workspace will no longer be a breeding-ground for disorder — a state which can lead only to inefficiency and dysfunction. In these rooms, observe the similar but contrasting approaches to shelving — one organic, one disciplined. Note, too, the way in which garden greenery makes a cameo appearance. In the room above, a vase of cut leaves naturalizes the workspace; while at left, a peephole penetrates the curved wall to allow a glimpse of nature whenever the observer takes the trouble to stand in exactly the right place to look out.

# a waterfall of steps and stairs

A change of level is usually the prelude to a new view. Stairs and steps may be solid or open – the difference between climbing a hill and climbing a ladder. But open stairs also become a screen which allows light to filter through while providing a framed vision of the view beyond. Taking just a few steps down into a room gives you a sense of enlarged space, and, as you bend your knees to descend, it is perhaps not too fanciful to suggest that you are performing a modest ceremony of genuflexion. Solid steps upward, on the other hand, allow you to rise both physically and spiritually in a manner that evokes an ascent toward the sky and, symbolically, toward enlightenment.

What is the waterfall
when you walk downstairs?
Is it the fall of time itself,
the flow of being?

# facing all ways

Sofas are places to let the taut watch-springs of mind and body unwind. They should be arranged for maximum versatility – people sitting apart, leaning toward each other in earnest dialogue, or even settling back to back on a single sofa to chat quietly. This room carries the sense that any kind of human

interaction could take place here – from dancing to having a lively debate about the meaning of time. Two aspects of the room are particularly noteworthy: first, how the rug defines a space within a space, and unifies the different elements; second, the way in which intimacy is created even though the open garden is brought so gloriously into the picture.

# angles and abstractions

"The light of the eyes like a comet,
and Zen's activity is like lightning.
The sword that kills
is the sword that saves."

*— Ekai*

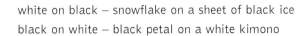

white on black — snowflake on a sheet of black ice
black on white — black petal on a white kimono

The yin-yang symbol of Daoism — two nestling commas in black and white — symbolizes a union of opposites. The effect of these tones is striking when used in a bold interior treatment. A black kimono, pinned against white on a black wall, adds depth to a narrow space, and provides a dramatic visual endstop. Although a deep shadow can always make a visual impact against white or cream, it is black on white that creates the most profound effect, gobbling light like a mythical light-eating dragon.

"Yellow tends so strongly to brightness that there cannot be such a colour as dark yellow. It may therefore be declared that there is a strong physical kinship between yellow and white."

— *Wassily Kandinsky*

# yellow

# a sense of two worlds

There is a special sense of privilege in a room that has windows on opposite walls — especially when the views are attractive on both sides. Where direct light from the sun streams in on one side, it meets its ally — the more diffuse light reflected in from the north — in a kind of mystical marriage. In this living room, the theme of window panes is taken up in a lighthearted way in the wall painting, with its irregular mesh of dark brushstrokes. Within this room, the space is fluid and

uncluttered, in a way that allows nothing to distract us from the inflow of light. We might see this openness and illumination as an image of Zen itself, breaking through the closed doors of the mind to let the light of truth flood the spirit. In the absence of such generously sized windows as these, another way to spread light more evenly within a room would be through judicious use of pale (and therefore reflective) wall surfaces, or strategically placed mirrors. Light should be welcomed into the home – or enticed if it seems reluctant.

LIVING

"No speck of dust anywhere.
 What's old? What's new?
 At home on my blue mountain,
 I want for nothing."
                        — *Shofu*

japanese boxes

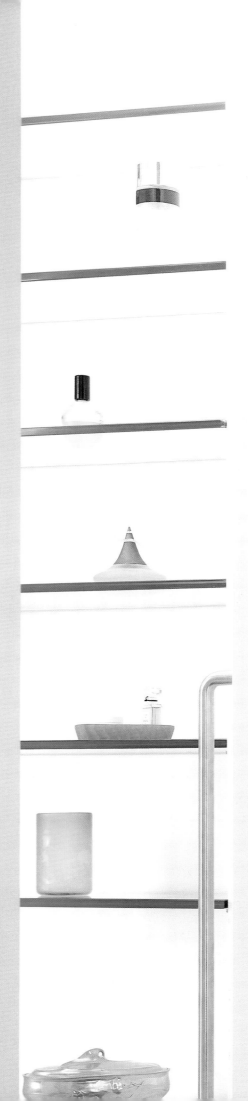

Zen emphasizes objects. Unless we pay attention to the shapes, colours and textures of the things that surround us, we are blind to the external world. An obvious expression of this attitude is to put interesting objects on display. Emphasize difference by placing them within a uniform framework – perhaps open wooden compartments or equally-spaced shelving. Try: seashells, pine cones, pebbles; or a group such as perfume bottles – you will be amazed at the variety within your chosen category if you take the trouble to look for new recruits.

In the Middle Ages Zen monks acted as scribes for the illiterate military rulers of Japan. Each had a low wooden writing desk called a *shoin*, built into an alcove. The *shoin* study alcove became an object of desire in the samurai household, reflecting the owner's intellectual aspirations. Soon an additional element was imported from the Zen monastery: the *tokonoma*. This was a built-in alcove, used to hold religious art for contemplation. Soon, however, it was secularized, and used to show flowers and small objects of art, sometimes from abroad, as well as scroll-paintings. Use your own alcove as a household shrine, with photos of loved ones on display, or perhaps miniature Buddhas or other Eastern statuettes.

# alcoves

"He who believes that nothingness
is formless, that flowers are visions –
let him enter boldly!"

– *Gido*

# tabletop nature

The eye is always ready to accept – indeed, welcome – natural things placed out of context. A miniature table-top landscape can be made of just a few ingredients. In the main picture here notice how the branches have the effect of standing in for, or symbolizing, a tree, while the grasses in their small containers represent the rest of the garden. The eye is always satisfied by miniature worlds. Instead of greenery you could take the same approach to pebbles or rocks. Dining indoors in such surroundings becomes almost an *al fresco* affair.

# character in plants

Plants in containers, used indoors, often have a presence that is disproportionate to their weight or volume. Above right, even the spindly branches make a major contribution to the overall look of the room. Still more weighty in their impact are the three fan-shaped houseplants (right), conveying an Eastern flavour without overstatement. The arum lilies above left hold their own against a busy background.

The fern in the corner of your living room
takes advantage of your picnicking
to grow a discernible fraction in private.

# outside inside

Outside is no more beyond us – that is, "out there" – than the rooms we live in: we inhabit nature too. Try to break down the artificial barriers that screen us from the natural world. To encourage this change of perspective, you might even bring a miniature garden indoors – the converse of setting up a formal dining table beside a sea of gravel.

In the world of nature
stone and water are non-existent.
The great round mirror of truth
has no preferences or aversions.

# ponds and rocks indoors

Water and rock, used indoors, offer a harmonious way to connect an interior to the exterior view beyond. The oval pool, left, bisected by the glass wall, is the focus of an ingenious transition, whose busyness, with pebbles and a little water cascade, contrasts with the plain wooden floor of the living room. The effect is to unite the inside with the outside, breaking down the boundaries of the expected. In the example on this page a slate desk serves a similar purpose, acting as foreground to the outdoor paving stones, and suggesting a home that embraces nature, while at the same time nature embraces the home. The same strategy, of course, could be applied to tree-trunk still lifes. Remember that the simplest indoor pool is just a water-filled bowl, perhaps with a pebble floor.

# sleeping

LIGHT, THE BEDROOM'S HONOURED GUEST.
A ROOM FOR AWAKENING. SLEEPING LOW.
COLOURS AND PATTERNS. THINGS IN THEIR
PLACE. A CONSTELLATION OF LEAVES. BATH,
BED AND BOARD.

"Awakening, I learn again the dance
    of the cherry blossom,
    the pleasant endless work of the mirror,
    the feel of sunlight."

— *Modern haiku*

The mood of a bedroom is an important contributory factor in the quality of our sleep. As we surrender consciousness, it is reassuring to know that we do so in an environment in which we can have faith – one with sympathetic energies. This means a room that is understated in its impact on the senses, where decorative features are handled with restraint. In planning the bedroom, we would do well to remember that this is the room that salutes us in the morning, as well as soothes us on our way to sleep at night. One crucial element, of course, is the lighting – not only the flexibility of artificial lighting for the evening, but the way in which natural light behaves in the room throughout the day, as it interacts with fabrics and reflective surfaces.

At its purest, the Zen bedroom has a low bed that seems not merely positioned on the floor, but profoundly connected with it – the written characters of the two words in Japanese are identical. Yet in the traditional Japanese home, the bed is a temporary resident. Sectioned by a screen, a bedroom is defined by the fact that a bed, usually a pure cotton futon, is laid within it at that moment. When the bed is removed and folded away, a daily occurrence each morning in Zen monasteries, the bedroom no longer exists. This small act of self-discipline strengthens the Zen monk spiritually. Making a bed in the Western manner can be regarded in a similar light – as a valuable miniature ceremony, reflecting attention to detail and respect for good order.

To aid your quality of sleep, it can help to arrange the room in ways that lend themselves to pre-sleep meditation. A single cut flower in a vase, for example, offers a possible subject for meditative practice, or you could use a calligraphic wall hanging to the same purpose.

# light, the bedroom's honoured guest

The bedroom is where we slip into the shadows of sleep, our "I" dissolving into emptiness. It is thus a very special room where, if the design is simple and pure, we can genuinely feel that we are close to the Zen Way. Pale, plain fabrics are hospitable to shadows and help to create an appropriate mood of fluidity and formlessness. We all know the sensation of staring into the half-light and being unable to distinguish solid from space, near from far. This is an experience to relish in the Zen bedroom. What is the point of complex patterns and flounces when at dawn and dusk their superficialities are drowned by subtle vagaries of light? Let light itself be your bedroom's honoured guest: attend patiently, with a calm, clear mind, as it brightens or fades like the mind itself drifting into and out of oblivion.

"A morning-glory at my window satisfies
me more than the metaphysics of books."
– *Walt Whitman*

# a room for awakening

The experience of awakening tends to be taken for granted: the alarm clock rings, a hand reaches out to silence it, and automatically we rise and start the day's business. But try to think of awakenings as more special than this. After all, our consciousness has come through a kind of re-birth, a small-scale miracle. Arrange your bedroom in ways that celebrate the wonder of this phenomenon. Give yourself something pleasurable and positive to wake up to. And try to wake up naturally, without mechanical aids – in due course you will soon find yourself rousing at a time to suit your daily routine. In the bedroom shown here, the sunray window has obvious connotations of dawn and positive energy; while the candlestick tripod harks back to the night through which we have slept. Waking up among shades of white is also symbolically appropriate: this is an innocent new day, which has yet to acquire the colours of experience.

# sleeping low

Ask a Zen adept why he should choose to sleep on a cotton floor pallet instead of a Western mattress, and he might answer that he needs to be closer to the earth. To lift sleep on a high platform, on an elaborate contrivance of springs, has a touch of artifice about it. Sleeping is a bodily function, and like all bodily functions should not be interfered with. Natural fibre mattresses have, in any event, been used for many thousands of years in the East. While the West has rejected them in favour of softer, springier beds, the cotton pallet, or futon, has thick, cotton cushioning which allows muscles to relax and skin to breathe naturally, while the firm, supportive surface ensures deep, undisturbed sleep. Cotton is renowned for its ability to

breathe, keeping the body fresh and cool in summer and providing warm insulation in winter. This flexibility is useful in a climate as extreme as that of Japan but, if any extra warmth and comfort are needed in winter, extra layers can always be added. The mattresses themselves require good ventilation and frequent shaking to prevent them from becoming matted and hard. Since space is used flexibly in Japan, the futon is a perfect solution. When day breaks, it is rolled up, along with pillows and blankets, and stowed away in a closet. A Japanese mattress would always be placed directly on a *tatami* mat, but Western futons tend to be used on low bases; in some designs the base folds to make a chair.

## colours and patterns

The cushions in the two views above, contributing bright accents of colour within a world of white, remind us that white light is the origin of the whole spectrum of hues. Dramatic tones add touches of visual drama that bring the whole room vibrantly to life. Colour punctuation-marks may seem the epitome of the Western approach to design, rather than reflecting the spirit of the East. Yet an intense dash of colour – like a spice added to a dish – is Zen-like in its concentrated individuality. Pattern, similarly, is not necessarily antithetical to Zen. The larger image here shows how a muted pattern adds visual interest to a fabric arrangement without distracting from subtle tonal effects. To modern eyes, a world that is entirely without pattern is a world in which imagination fails to make its full contribution.

Having a place for clothes, linen and towels, and a system for managing them, is a necessary part of the Zen lifestyle. *Shibui*, a fundamental part of Zen philosophy, implies, among other things, the strength of self-discipline, and the absence of all that is inessential. An extreme version of this concept would be to have only as many clothes as you need, and to give away an old item every time you buy a new one. But,

# things in their place

whatever management system you choose to follow, the Zen way is always to take pleasure in order. Place all shoes in baskets, pockets or wardrobe compartments. Store all shirts together on a rail. Fold sweaters neatly together in colour batches. What is hidden should be no less tidy than what is on display – just as the gracefulness of outward behaviour has no depth unless there is grace within.

# a constellation of leaves

There is always something mysteriously appealing about a cluster or family of motifs — the whole is greater than the sum of the parts. Here, silvered artificial maple-leaves hang above the bed like a constellation of stars, pouring a benevolent radiance of good fortune down upon the sleeper. You could, of course, use star shapes in a similar way, but the effect would be weaker. Zen looks for the similarities between different aspects of nature, and rejoices in the parallels. In this example, the double reference to stars and leaves gives the effect of someone sleeping out, among trees under a glorious night sky. The silver also hints at moonlight.

"On rainy leaves —
the glow
of the village lights."
— *Ryota*

"No need to shave my head again, or wash.
Just set the firewood flaming – that's enough."
– *9th-century Zen text*

Opening an en-suite bathroom into the bedroom itself, with no screening, has all the unexpectedness of Zen – a willingness to look at the conventions of use and privacy and question whether there is any benefit in overturning them. In this room (shown from two different viewpoints) the advantages of this radical approach to planning are a pleasing fluidity in the disposition of space and the option of increased sociability. In the Zen esthetic the boundaries between private and public spheres are always blended in this way. In the architecture of

# bath, bed and board

the Zen house, indeed, there is frequently no separate bedroom, or even bathroom. All space is communal; all rooms are interchangeable; and all bath-times are, theoretically, for the entire family. This reflects a view of life that refuses to accept privileged treatment for any individual when it comes to bodily functions. In the bathhouse we are all equal. To insist on absolute privacy for bathtime is to surround the ego with self-protective measures that belong more to a Western than to an Eastern philosophy. Of course, as with all Zen notions, Westerners need not follow such disciplines too slavishly.

# cleansing

WINDOW WATERFALLS. LIGHT ON WATER. THE
BARE TRUTH OF WHITE. A CLEAR CUBE OF
WATER. NATURAL BEAUTY.

Water starts high in the mountains —
higher, in the clouds.
Like the seasons it comes into our homes
and sustains life.

Zen attaches fundamental importance to our link with nature. Water is the vital element, in many ways the life-giver of the earth. And washing is an engagement with that element, in the form of a symbolic purification. There is a reverence in cleanliness, linked to the respect we owe to our own bodies and to the idea of ablutions as a small-scale domestic act of thanksgiving, as well as to that most profound and mysterious of meetings – sleep.

In the Zen-style bathroom, functionalism will usually be to the fore. Paradoxically, although such plainness is a bulwark against the distractions of ostentatious luxury, the spare style is austerely beautiful. In the West the spirit of Zen might move us to make the bathroom a place where we may enjoy subtle esthetic satisfactions – not self-denial exactly, nor self-indulgence, but somehow a state of truthfulness and repose that is not achievable in quite the same way in any other room. Surrounded by refined textures, colour tones and shadowy filtered light, we may enter, as we shower or bathe, a state akin to meditation.

The spiritual value of cleansing is twofold. First, there is a psychological effect of grounding the spirit, relaxing us into harmony with the elements. Secondly, and most importantly, bathing itself becomes a ritual. Repeated within a daily routine, washing and cleansing amount to a literal and symbolic act of regeneration. Implied in these tasks is a combination of humility and self-respect.

Dogen, the thirteenth-century Zen master, taught that awareness can be found in action as well as meditation. While devoting ourselves to cleansing, we take positive spiritual nourishment from mindfulness – a total alertness, with all the senses, to the experience of the moment.

The shades in the bathroom opposite and above left can be thought, without too much stretching of the imagination, as waterfalls — art imitating nature in the Zen way. A variation on this idea is the blue-tinted glass washbasin, above right, which we perceive as a pool at the foot of a waterfall. These hints of nature, although extremely subtle, are enough to work a gentle healing magic upon the mind. The sound effects of rain beyond the window would amplify this effect, giving an aural dimension to the visual reference.

Rain starts:
soon waterfalls become the leitmotif of the streets' music.

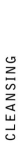

The ruling spirit of the bathroom
is gravity.
Gravity allied with water
serves our need to be cleansed.

# window waterfalls

# light on water

When light touches water, we are privileged to
witness miracles;
when light, flowers and water come together,
we have a glimpse of paradise.

The bathroom, provided it has a window, brings together two elements of nature: light and water. One approach to design is to maximize the possibilities for interaction between the two. The main picture here shows a stone washbasin with flowerheads floating in a shallow dip. The eye adjusts its sense of scale when confronted by such miniature landscapes: we are drawn in. There is a part of the human spirit that wants every water surface to be a lake or an ocean. You could float seventeen flowerheads in such a basin – each corresponding to one of the syllables of the traditional haiku. Both pictures show light as a backdrop – a hint of the infinity that lies beyond.

# the bare truth of white

White is the resolution of all colours – the purity at the heart of all we see. White bathrooms yield full sovereignty to shadows and tones. Far from being austere, they open up a sensual kingdom which the Zen mind sees as an extravaganza of beautiful perceptions. The two bathrooms pictured here show contrasting approaches to Zen design. One, with its rough textures, invites you to touch and therefore to use. You can imagine the feel of the towels and the touch of your hand against the brickwork as you step out of the bath. This is a tactile bathroom – appropriate to Zen because Zen embraces the reality and importance of roughness. But light is Zen too.

The second bathroom is a composition in light, like a vision. There is an air of reverence also – the bath is treated like an altar, evoking the holiness and rightness of bathing. White bathrooms such as these lend themselves well to bath-time meditations. Sit or lie comfortably in your bath and look at the many shades of white, flowing into each other. Distinguish between these shades in your mind. Then let go of the distinctions you have made and welcome into your perceptions the seamlessness of one tone or shade flowing into the next. Think of this flow as a kind of mental balm, filling your mind with milky peace. The world's clashing colours are here resolved into a Zen perfection.

# a clear cube of water

The Japanese bath, or *furo*, is used by more than one person at a time. Its prime function is not cleansing (this takes place in a quick shower before entering the tub) but relaxation. The bathtub illustrated here conforms to Japanese tradition only in being roomy enough for two. However, it is Zen-like in its purity of design. With its angled positioning, transparent sides and invisible plumbing, it defies the conventions of bathrooms in the same way that a Zen koan, or paradoxical parable, defies the logic of reason.

# natural beauty

Zen has a preference for rough surfaces, for natural materials, for objects that immediately announce their use. It can be enjoyable to furnish a bathroom following these principles. As well as the obvious functional items, you might consider small-scale sculptural touches as well — for example, driftwood. Zen delights in simple but ingenious solutions to everyday problems — the soap on a folded openweave cloth wrapped around a block of wood in a bowl as in the second picture here is a

"Chrysanthemums
bloom ... amid the stones
of the stone-yard."
— *Basho*

good example: see if you can devise your own little inventions in the same spirit. Looked at close up, many bathroom accessories that make use of natural materials have surprising textural qualities. Fascinating textures for bathrooms include: natural sponges, braided and plaited ropes and straw, and the craggier kinds of stoneware. In a subtle way these rough surfaces suggest a disciplined purification of the body — a willingness not to cosset ourselves too much with the self-indulgent lotions of the pharmacy.

# eating

THE ZEN KITCHEN. EVERYTHING IN ITS PLACE.
STONE STEEL WOOD WATER HEAT LIGHT. PLACE
SETTINGS. FRESHNESS. RICE. A BOWL OF NOODLES.
STEAM FRY GRILL BOIL. THE VEGETABLE FEAST.
A SALAD OF FLOWERS. FRUITS. SEAWEED.
SUSHI AND SASHIMI. THE TEA CEREMONY. THE
INTIMATE OUTDOORS.

"When you prepare vegetables or soup, don't
worry — just prepare them with sincerity."
— *Dogen*

As with many of life's daily activities, Zen regards eating as providing spiritual as well as bodily nourishment. Choosing, preparing, serving and consuming food have a special importance in Zen, offering us the opportunity to show, in the ways in which these activities are performed, a sensitivity to what really matters in life – if food, our fundamental fuel, is not worth honouring with care and skill, why should we bother with our environment? To lavish taste and thought on interior design, and not upon mealtimes, would strike the Zen-tutored mind as a gross anomaly. Moreover, neglecting the art of good cooking (or any other aspect of lifestyle) would prompt dark forebodings as to how well we might be expected to care for the spirit.

The esthetic values of well-presented food are a prime concern in Zen, yet this is only the endpoint of a whole, rich, mindful experience that starts in the market or garden and ends with clearing up after the last guest's last goodbye echoes on the threshold. Which brings us, of course, to the social aspects of cooking. In devoting ourselves to the pleasure and wellbeing of others, we grow in spiritual stature. A convivial meal of light, flavoursome food is one of the highest expressions of civilized values.

To serve the health requirements of the body is to provide an excellent grounding for the life of the spirit. Zen leans toward a pure, refined diet, whose fundamental principles have been followed for centuries – but which strikes us today, in the light of modern science, as exceptionally cleansing and healthy. Meals served in a Zen monastery will be vegetarian, as the most austere practitioners will not take their protein from animals. Food types are carefully balanced. Bean curd, also known as tofu, is the main protein block. Fragrant rice will always accompany the main dish. The clear, sharp flavour of aromatic miso soup is also favoured. For many the most eagerly awaited dish is sashimi, or raw fish. Fish must only ever be caught in season, then finely sliced by a chef dedicated to the ritualistic art of sushi. Freshness is of supreme importance for all food.

What is known in the West as a macro-biotic diet upholds the Zen principles of harmony, wholeness and balance. Yet such an approach to cookery is not merely designed to provide optimal nutrition and fresh flavour. The meal must also educate and please the Zen mind. It does this through an understated chemistry of ingredients, with finely individual textures, subtle colourings and delicate flavours. But not least of the meal's vital properties is its visual presentation. Once the chef has finished in the kitchen, his main responsibility is to select plates and bowls that display the food at its best. Over centuries this matching of tableware to foodstuffs has developed into a creative art – the simplicity of raw fish heightened with a base of bare wood, a plain, white rice roll dramatically set off against dark lacquerware. But as a matter of principle, a great chef will never repeat exactly the same arrangement.

The moment of bringing food to the mouth might be sanctified by appropriate observations. Before taking the first mouthful, think of the food as the fruit of earth and sun – a key link to the vital sources of our energy. While gazing in anticipation at a full plate, be sure to recall the hunger of the less fortunate. Cultivate the seeds of compassion. The lunch or dinner table is no place to forget our connections with humanity at large.

# the zen kitchen

What makes a good Zen kitchen? There are several key factors. One is harmony in the arrangement of parts, a good practical circulation route that allows tasks to be performed efficiently, and a clear decision as to what is to be hidden and what is to be left on display. Surfaces will be allowed to make their own statement, and will either be natural or visually pure, as steel is. None of the peripheral clutter that is found in most Western kitchens will appear – calendars, postcards, refrigerator magnets, randomly thrown together, are all inimical to the spirit of Zen.

# everything in its place

In an all-white kitchen, Zen purism is brought to the working heart of the home. In this example to the left, the strategy is one of undisguised functionalism. Neatly arranged in individually labelled compartments, mundane items of equipment present themselves shamelessly to public view – even a humble bucket. All is as it should be, except the clock, which is tilted – a Zen paradox about time (clock time after all is a human invention: if time slips out of true, why should it cloud our minds with anxiety?). It may seem impossibly idealistic to keep all your kitchen artifacts on show like this – making minute positional changes every time you put a kitchen implement back in its place. However, you could always cheat by having cupboards as well, for all your everyday equipment. Note the well-positioned flexible clamp-light to illuminate the cooking area. Observe also the practicality of having a built-in cutting board directly next to the stove.

The kitchen has a clear purpose: the storage, preparation, cooking and serving of food. Organize your kitchen around these essentials. To use excessive ornament in the kitchen is to decorate a mountain stream with coloured paints. Steel and wood speak of themselves, the shine and grain of reality. Dwell in the world, not in the mind.

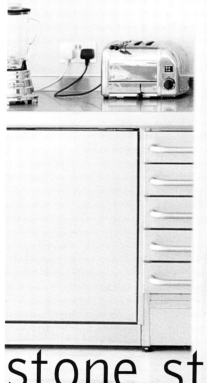

stone steel wood

"'A monk asked a Zen Master, 'What is the meaning of Zen?' The Master in turn asked, 'Have you had breakfast?' 'Yes,' said the monk. 'Then wash your bowl,' said the Master.''
                                                                    – *Mu mon*

water heat light

The roundness of plate or bowl —
a world within a world.
Everything we are and do is framed by
the circle of eternity.

place settings

Yield to a salad of leaves and flowers all passions, all desires of the heart.

To cook in the Zen way is to work simply, happily and methodically, with the best and freshest ingredients you can find, not getting anxious or annoyed about the amount or quality of the food. Work in such a way that the ingredients, for as long as you are handling them, are real and present in your mind, in all their qualities; and your mind is real and present in the ingredients. Be aware of the feast for the senses that even the preparation of food offers, before you bring a single morsel to your mouth.

# freshness

# rice

Rice is the building-block of the Zen diet. In a monastery, even a single meal without rice is unthinkable. Japanese rice is short-grain, snowy white, and sticky when cooked (an effect easily achieved in a rice cooker) – although extreme ascetics would have eaten the brown (unhulled) variety. Centuries ago this grain was used as a measure of wealth by the samurai. The taste of plain, boiled rice is the ideal backdrop for Zen food – allowing the flavours of the rest

of the ingredients to come to the fore. Rice is arguably at its best with simple Japanese light soy sauce and bright-green chopped spring onions for flavour and crunch. However, the Japanese also snack on rice balls wrapped in *nori* (seaweed), sometimes with pickles, fish or other food in the centre. *Mochi* rice cakes are made by pounding glutinous rice in a wooden mortar: the chewy round cakes are either eaten as they are, or toasted lightly. Commercially made *mochi* cakes are sold in Japanese food stores.

# a bowl of noodles

Brownish soba (buckwheat) and white udon (wheat flour) noodles are staples of the Japanese diet; there is also a variety called *cha-shoba*, made with green tea. The fact that noodles are so common-place increases rather than undermines their appeal. We rejoice in such simple food as we rejoice in air and sunlight. Always buy fresh noodles if available — refrigerate, unopened, until ready for use. Serve in a bowl whose roundness symbolizes harmony.

# steam fry grill boil

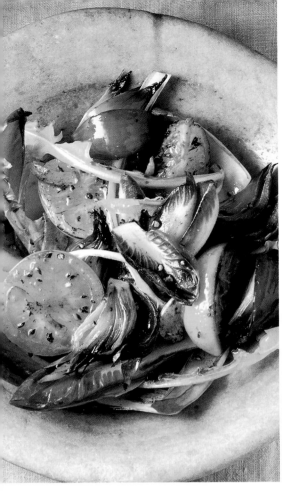

**Miso soup**

There are many variations on this hearty dish. It is actually very difficult to make a miso soup that does not taste delicous.

Dilute the miso with a little *dashi* (seaweed-based) stock, simmer, then add more stock, and continue simmering. Add tofu in little cubes. Serve hot in a lacquered bowl with finely-chopped spring onion.

In line with the importance of serving food as freshly as possible, to rejoice in its vibrant colours and flavours, cooking methods in the Zen monastery or household are kept as plain as possible. A Chinese bamboo steamer is a fine way to cook every sort of vegetable while preserving its nutrients, shape and texture. A favourite simple meal layers steamed green leaves, such as pak choi, with scarlet and orange bell peppers drizzled with light Japanese soy sauce and nut oil and sprinkled with toasted seeds. In modern Japan, fried food is a more healthy option than its Western counterpart, as vegetable oil is always used, and the fried fish or meat is invariably accompanied by fresh, often raw vegetables; try deep-fried tempura tiger prawns laid asymmetrically over oak lettuce leaves with an aromatic dip. Meat and fish are often grilled, sealing in natural juices; *teriyaki* trout has the fish scored, skewered and marinated in soy and *mirin* (wine) sauce before grilling it at high heat. Boiling is reserved for soups: miso stock with simmered steak cubes, shiitake mushrooms and mangetouts makes a filling but light, clear broth.

# the vegetable feast

Garden-fresh green and root vegetables are a cornerstone of the Zen diet. Every vegetable is served either raw or lightly cooked, which not only maintains its full nutritional value and preserves the subtlety of flavour so essential to Zen, but also, by keeping our food closer to its natural state, reinforces links with the cycles of growth around us. While cooking methods may appear simple, much of the delight in Zen food lies in the supreme artistry of its presentation and serving. Exquisite, often unusual and witty, arrangements are nothing less than edible art; which, in its beauty, raises us above the merely mundane routine of bodily sustenance to high levels of delight and mindfulness.

# a salad of flowers

There is something typically Zen about the idea of adding flower petals to food, as an edible garnish. Fruit and vegetable flowers complete a satisfying circle when paired with the obviously edible parts of the same plant. Many flowers are toxic; and all composite flowers (that is, multi-petalled flowers such as the daisy) have highly allergenic pollen and should be avoided altogether by hayfever and asthma sufferers. Do not eat flower petals unless you know they are safe and tasty – the list opposite gives some suggestions. Pick blooms in the morning and refrigerate in an air-tight container.

## Some edible flowers

*Chrysanthemum* 'Garland' (*C. coronarium*): bitter, pungent (beware: the pollen-bearing
  flower-centres are allergenic)

Carnations (*Dianthus caryophyllus*): spicy, peppery, clove-like

Dandelion (*Taraxacum officinalis*): fried in butter, the buds taste like mushrooms

Day lily (*Hemerocallis* species): sweet and crunchy like lettuce, tasting of chestnuts
  (note: many *Lilium* species are toxic)

Lemon blossom (*Citrus limon*): distinctive flavour, use sparingly as a garnish

Nasturtiums (*Tropaeolum majus*): slightly peppery; the leaves taste of cress

Rose petals (*Rosa* species): delicately flavoured, often used on desserts; try crystallized petals
  or entire miniature flowerheads

Scented geranium (*Pelargonium* species): a range of spicy and citrus flavours

Borage (*Borago officinalis*): lovely star-shaped blooms with a taste like cucumber

Marigold (*Calendula officinalis*): the orange variety is used as a substitute for saffron
  in rice and soup

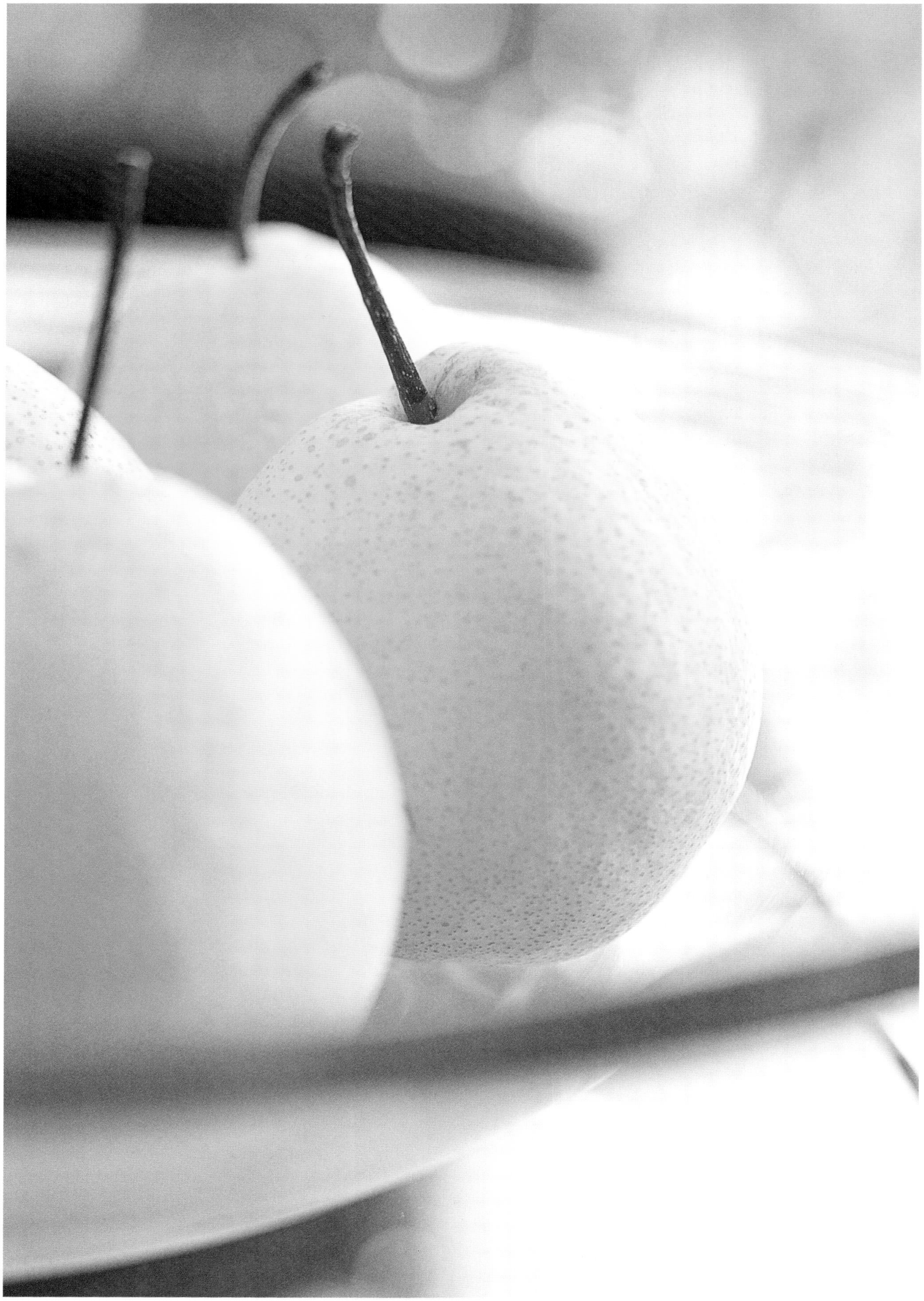

# fruits

Fruits bring together whole clusters of symbolism in a way that heightens the joyous experience of eating them. Their juicy deliciousness links them with a pleasure in the world's blessings, and yet this pleasure is soon over – which makes us think of the transience of all experience, the loss of the fleeting moment. That the peach, in China, is a symbol of immortality thus becomes a fascinating paradox. Eat fresh fruits for breakfast and as an appetizer before other meals. Try to find a reliable supplier of organic fruits and vegetables. Fresh fruits should be firm, colourful and "alive", and buying in season will provide a further link with the cycles of nature.

On seeing peach blossom, the monk Lin yun immediately gained enlightenment.

In various cultures pomegranates (like gourds, oranges and other many-seeded fruits) are symbols of fertility, abundance, love and marriage. In China this fruit is one of the Three Blessed Fruits of Buddhism. Throughout Asia the image of a pomegranate split into two and hinged apart conveys good wishes. Usually served alone on a white porcelain dish and cut simply, pomegranates should only be eaten in their late summer season. Serve with aromatic green tea.

Cherries are a samurai emblem, the symbol of the warrior's calling, and the destiny that lies in wait for him. These associations may derive from the image of a hard kernel within blood-coloured skin and flesh. Dark red, in China, is a symbol of the soul and immortality. Most Japanese cherries are grown for their blossom, not their fruit. However, edible cherries have an intensity of colour that gives them an appealing role in any Zen table arrangement.

# seaweed

Used in savoury dishes for centuries by the island-dwellers of Japan, the numerous varieties of edible seaweed feature in many different forms throughout historic and modern Japanese cookery. Surprisingly easy to prepare, seaweed is rich in the B vitamins that support our nervous system. This ancient "mood food" is sold in four popular forms. *Konbu*, or kelp, is used to flavour stock; you might also try it powdered and sprinkled on various dishes. Dark sheets of *konbu* may be

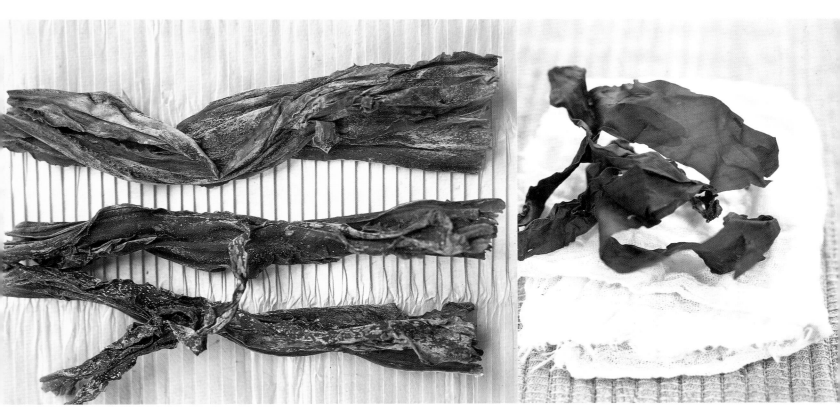

laid beneath steamed sweet potato, turnip and artichoke to highlight their colours and shapes. The dried black fronds of *hijiki* are soaked for salads or floated in creamed tofu soups. *Wakame*, or "lobe leaf", is sold in dried form: mixed with water it turns bright green. Perhaps the commonest and best-known variety is *nori*, the blue-black, tissue-thin sheets of seaweed that wrap sushi with a delicate, marine tang. Dried *nori* should be freshened by toasting lightly. Crumbled *nori* is sold in small bottles, like pepper shakers, for seasoning.

EATING

Characteristically Japanese, sushi (small rice cakes) and sashimi (sliced raw fish) – often served together – are recognized for their nutritional value, flavour and delicacy throughout the West. Prepared with a complementary dipping sauce, there is barely a single fish or shellfish in marine or inland waters that cannot be made into sashimi. If you live far from the coast and do not have access to really fresh sea fish (absolute freshness is crucial), then try freshwater varieties. The Japanese often make a sashimi rose out of a fresh raw tuna fillet – by cutting and rolling they transform the fish into an imitation flower bud, perhaps with a dab of *wasabi* horseradish in the centre. You might decorate such a rose with real rose leaves around the outside. Sushi, of course, has become the healthy fast food of our times – to avoid monotony, think of unusual accompaniments.

# sushi and sashimi

When we have a true sense of ourselves in the moment of drinking tea, at that moment, life is.

# the tea ceremony

The tea ceremony, or *cha no yu*, was developed centuries ago by the Zen master Sen no Rikyu. Following detailed rules that can be transmitted only from master to disciple, the art takes hours of study and practice to perfect. Invited into a tea-room with a log fire, guests enter through a Zen garden and, one at a time, rinse their mouths and hands with water from a stone basin. Each then sips the bitter, green tea while the host, who does not drink, focuses on simmering the water, whisking the tea and ladling it correctly. Drinking vessels are shared — enhancing the sense of community. The exquisite tea bowl, or *chawan*, is appreciated for its intrinsic beauty.

# the intimate outdoors

The social courtesies of Zen belong to the patio as much as to the dining room. Table settings are simple but ceremonious — perhaps with a symbolic gift for each guest. A herb or flower-head from the garden, like the lavender here, right, extends kindness and friendship to each participant — giving each person something to take away as a memento of a companionable interlude. It is at night that outdoor eating acquires its greatest intimacy, thanks largely to the pools of light created by lanterns or garden candles. The darkness outside the magic illuminated ring of ceremony and grace only serves to heighten the effect of a special gathering — a charmed circle of intimates creating their own version of civilization amid the impenetrable mysteries of the night. White table linen, in such circumstances, is especially apt and impressive. And luxurious silverware and faceted crystal glassware will catch the lanternlight or candle-light and contribute their own memorable grace-notes to the scene.

# index

# acknowledgments

The publishers would like to thank the following individuals and organizations for their kind permission to reproduce the illustrations listed below.

1 Paul Ryan/International Interiors/designer Jacqueline Morabito; 3 Garden Picture Library/Mark Bolton 5 Camera Press/Fair Lady 6 left Camera Press/Fair Lady 6 centre Trip/D Harding 6 right Taverne Agency/Hotze Eisma/Rianne Landstra 7 left Axiom/James Morris/Hempel Design 7 centre Paul Ryan/International Interiors 7 right Gettyone Stone/Victoria Pearson 8 Ray Main/Mainstream/designer Kelly Hoppen; 9 Marie Claire Maison/Yutaka Yamamoto/Marion Bayle 10 above left Ou Baholyodhin 10 above right Ou Baholyodhin 10 below left Ou Baholyodhin 10 below right Ou Baholyodhin 11 Ou Baholyodhin 12 above Ou Baholyodhin 12 below Ou Baholyodhin 13 Ou Baholyodhin 14 Camera Press/Fair Lady 15 © Living/Paul Grootes 20 Trip/D Harding 21 Impact Photos/Harvey Male 24 Gettyone Stone/Peter Samuels 28 Trip/Christopher Rennie 29 Arcaid/Ian Lambot 30 Axiom/James Morris/Hempel Design 31 Axiom/architect John Pawson 32 Houses & Interiors/Verne 33 Richard Glover/architect John Pawson 36–37 Elizabeth Whiting & Associates/Di Lewis 40 © VT Wonen/Paul Grootes 41 IPC International Syndication/Hannah Lewis/© Homes & Gardens 42–43 Axiom/Kutomi 44 Trip/D Harding 45 Jacqui Hurst 50 Ray Main/Mainstream 51 Undine Pröhl 52–53 Elizabeth Whiting & Associates/Neil Lorimer 54–55 Gettyone Stone 55 Gettyone Stone/Ernst Haas 56 left Andrew Lawson 56 right Elizabeth Whiting & Associates 57 Impact Photos/Mark Henley 58 Gettyone Stone/David Muench 59 above Arcaid/Ian Lambot 59 below Axiom/Jim Holmes 60 Andrew Lawson 61 Andrew Lawson/Newby Hall, Yorks 62 Garden Picture Library/Ron Sutherland 62 inset Elizabeth Whiting & Associates 63 above Axiom/Luke White 63 below Clive Nichols/designer Trevyn McDowell & Paul Thompson 64 Jerry Harpur/Wave Hill, New York 64–65 The Interior Archive/Helen Fickling/artist Prinsloo 65 Reiner Blunck/architects David Morton & Thomas Cordell 66 IPC International Syndication/© Amateur Gardening 67 left IPC International Syndication/William Shaw/© Amateur Gardening 67 right IPC International Syndication/© Amateur Gardening 68–69 Gettyone Stone/Rosemary Calvert 69 Robert O'Dea 70 Gettyone Stone/Paul Wakefield 71 above Collections/Ashley Cooper 71 below Gettyone Stone/Dietrich Rose 72–73 Garden Picture Library/John Glover 74 Garden Picture Library/Steven Wooster 75 above Marie Claire Maison/André Martin/Mathilde Trebucq 75 centre Gettyone Stone/Renée Lynn 75 below Andrew Lawson 76 Andrew Lawson 77 Jerry Harpur/designer Terry Welch 78 above Gettyone Stone 78 below Garden Picture Library/Frank Leather 79 Gettyone Stone/Dan Gair 80 Taverne Agency/Hotze Eisma/Rianne Landstra 81 Ray Main/Mainstream/architect Mark Guard 86–87 Ray Main/Mainstream/designer Vincent Wolfe 88 above left The Interior Archive/Andrew Wood 88 above right The Interior Archive/Andrew Wood 88 below Jacqui Hurst 89 The Interior Archive/Simon Upton 90–91 View/Chris Gascoigne/architects Gerrard Taylor Associates 91 above Axiom/Luke White 91 below The Interior Archive/Fritz von der Schulenburg/designer De Padova 92 left Camera Press/IMS 92 right Impact Photos/Christophe Bluntzer 93 The Interior Archive/Ken Hayden/designer Jonathan Reed 94 View/Chris Gascoigne/architects Stanton Williams 95 Maison Madame Figaro/Philippe Costes 96 above Christian Sarramon 96 below Elizabeth Whiting & Associates 97 Arcaid/Richard Bryant/architect Spencer Fung 98–99 Christian Sarramon/designer Jacqueline Morabito 100–101 Ray Main/Mainstream/architect Simon Condor 102–103 Paul Ryan/International Interiors/architects Hariri & Hariri 103 The Interior Archive/Fritz von der Schulenburg/designer De Padova 104 Axiom/James Morris/architect Pip Horne 105 View/Peter Cook 106–107 The Interior Archive/Fritz von der Schulenburg/designer De Padova 108 Arcaid/Richard Glover/architect John Pawson 109 above Arcaid/Richard Glover/architect John Pawson 109 below Richard Glover/architect Arthur Collin 110 Axiom/Heidi Grassley/Hempel Design 111 left Christian Sarramon/J de Meulder, Anvers 111 right Christian Sarramon/Paris, Henri Becq 112 Narratives/Jan Baldwin 113 above Elizabeth Whiting & Associates/Lu Jeffery 113 below Christian Sarramon/Simoen 114 Ray Main/Mainstream/designer Ben de Lisi 115 Ray Main/Mainstream 116–117 Ray Main/Mainstream/Nick Allan Design 118 View/Peter Cook/architect Jonathan Woolf 119 Nadia Mackenzie 120 above Elizabeth Whiting & Associates/Lu Jeffery 120 below Trip/H Rogers 121 Ray Main/Mainstream 122–123 Paul Ryan/International Interiors/architect Deborah Berke 123 Paul Ryan/International Interiors/architect David Ling 124 left Arcaid/Richard Bryant/architects Sergio Puente & Ada Dewes 124 right View/Peter Cook/Farnsworth House, architect Ludwig Mies van der Rohe 125 © Eigen Huis & Interieur/Dennis Brandsma 126–127 Marie Claire Maison/Bertrand Limbour/Catherine Ardouin 128 above Christian Sarramon/Buenos Aires, Luis Martorano 128 below Arcaid/Nicholas Kane/architects Shahriar Nasser 129 Axiom/Jim Holmes 130 Axiom/James Morris/Hempel Design 131 Ray Main/Mainstream/John Minshaw Designs 134–135 Paul Ryan/International Interiors/designer Jacqueline Morabito 137 Marie Claire Maison/Antoine Rozes/Veronique Normand 138 Elizabeth Whiting & Associates/Tim Street-Porter 139 Axiom/Heidi Grassley/Hempel Design 140 IPC International Syndication/© Living Etc./Lucy Pope 141 Ray Main/Mainstream 141 Houses & Interiors/Verne 142 left IPC International Syndication/© Homes & Gardens/James Merrell 142 right IPC International Syndication/© Ideal Home/David Giles 143 left Camera Press/Schöner Wohnen 143 right Richard Glover/Circus Architects 144–145 Ray Main/Mainstream/architect Mark Guard 146 above Arcaid/Petrina Tinsley/designers Phil & Jackie Staub 146 below Arcaid/Petrina Tinsley/designers Phil & Jackie Staub 148 Paul Ryan/International Interiors/designer Jacqueline Morabito 149 Elizabeth Whiting & Associates/Mark Luscombe-White 152 left Arcaid/Willem Rethmeier/Belle 152 right Houses & Interiors/Steve Hawkins/Teresa Ward 153 Axiom/Heidi Grassley/Hempel Design 154 Undine Pröhl 154–155 Paul Ryan/International Interiors/designer Jacqueline Morabito 156 Marie Claire Maison/Bertrand Limbour/Catherine Ardouin 157 Ray Main/Mainstream/Nick Allan Design 158–159 Paul Ryan/International Interiors/designers Kastrup & Sjunnesson 160 left Ray Main/Mainstream 160 right Ray Main/Mainstream 161 left Houses & Interiors/Steve Hawkins/Teresa Ward 161 right IPC International Syndication/©Homes & Ideas/David Giles 162 Gettyone Stone/Victoria Pearson 163 Paul Ryan/International Interiors/designer Michael Seibert 168 Arcaid/Earl Carter/Belle/architect Stephen Varady 169 left Richard Glover/designer Malin Iovino 169 right Undine Pröhl 170–171 Maison Madame Figaro/Nicolas Tosi/designer Jacqueline Morabito 171 Marie Claire Maison/Christoph Kicherer/Marie Kalt 172 Jacqui Hurst 172–173 The Interior Archive/Andrew Wood/designer David Edgell 174 Marie Claire Maison/Yutaka Yamamoto/Marion Bayle 175 Alexander van Berge 176 Jacqui Hurst 177 left Jacqui Hurst 177 right Jacqui Hurst 178 IPC International Syndication/Jean Cazals/© Family Circle 179 IPC International Syndication/Sandra Lane/© Country Homes & Interiors 180 The Interior Archive/Simon Upton/designer Marja Walters 181 IPC International Syndication/© Essentials/Ken Field 182 Camera Press/Brigitte 183 above Gettyone Stone/Laurie Evans 183 below Axiom/Paul Quayle 184 above Jacqui Hurst 184 below Jacqui Hurst 185 Insight/Jack Townsend 185 inset Ray Main/Mainstream 186 Garden Picture Library/David Cavagnaro 187 Ray Main/Mainstream 188 Ray Main/Mainstream 189 left Jean Cazals 189 right Anthony Blake Photo Library/Matthew May 190 Camera Press/Brigitte 191 Garden Picture Library/Mayer/Le Scanff 192 left Jean Cazals 192 right Jean Cazals 193 left Jean Cazals 193 right Jean Cazals 194 Jean Cazals 195 Jean Cazals 196 © Living/Paul Grootes 197 left Camera Press/Fair Lady 197 right Camera Press/SHE 198 Camera Press/Fair Lady 199 Camera Press/Fair Lady 200 above The Interior Archive/Thomas Stewart 200 below © VT Wonen/Paul Grootes 201 © Living/Paul Grootes 202 Jerry Harpur/designer Luciana Giubbelei; 203 IPC International Syndication/© Homes & Gardens/James Merrell

## Publishers' acknowledgments

The Publishers would like to thank the following for translations from the Chinese, Japanese, and other foreign-language texts: Dr Carl Maraspini; Susan Renshaw; Dr Benedict Stolling. Displayed texts not inside inverted commas have been specially devised for this volume.

For information on the work and designs of Ou Baholyodhin, readers may visit his website at the following location: www.ou-b.com.